STONEHENGE

A report into the civil liberties implications of the events relating to the convoys of summer 1985 and 1986

National Council for Civil Liberties

National Council for Civil Liberties,
21 Tabard Street, London SE1 4LA

ISBN 0 946088 28 4

Typeset, printed and bound in Great Britain by
The Yale Press Ltd, London SE25 5LY

Contents

Acknowledgements

NCCL observers should be thanked first for their meticulous and objective recording of events and their tenacity in staying with the convoy despite often inhospitable weather conditions. They include those who were present 20 - 22 June 1985, at Stoney Cross in Wiltshire on 9th June 1986 and 19 - 22 June 1986 continuously, and sporadically at other periods.

In our observations, we saw at first hand the dedicated work of the Festival Welfare Services in providing welfare, help and assistance for members of the convoy. Similarly, Release provided effective and efficient legal back-up for travellers. Many individuals in the Salisbury area helped us with food, accommodation and transport over this period and in particular we would like to thank Tish Seabourne and local Quakers.

The research for this period was carried out by Katy Ferguson, and Bill Forrester contributed the information on which the section on the Caravan Sites Act is based.

Thanks are also due to Paddy Hillyard and Alex Carlile QC MP of NCCL's executive committee, Sarah Spencer, NCCL's General Secretary, and Peter Thornton as well as Jane Goodsir from Release, the Festival Welfare Services, Tim Greene, solicitor, Maggie Whiteley and Nettie Pollard for reading and commenting on the manuscript within a very short space of time. Carolyn Hartley and Victoria Teggin typed the manuscript with great speed and efficiency and John Myers published the report within three working days of receiving the completed manuscript.

The legal sections of the report owe much to Peter Thornton, who generously gave us access to the manuscript of his forthcoming book, 'Public Order Law' to be published by Financial Training Publications Ltd. upon which we have drawn heavily for the sections on the law. Tim Greene of Birnbergs, Solicitors, kindly provided essential information about the civil law background to these events. Thanks generally are due to Birnberg & Co. for their continued help and co-operation.

Marie Staunton
June 1986

Introduction

The movement of travellers towards Stonehenge at the time of the summer solstice has become an annual feature of West Country life. While the Home Secretary has described the members of the convoy as 'medieval brigands', and Margaret Thatcher said in June 1986 that she would 'make life difficult for such things as hippy convoys', and senior police officers have developed strategies to 'neutralise' them and describe them as 'pollution', others have marvelled at the level of intolerance shown to a small group of people who have adopted an alternative life style, exemplified by police tactics such as dawn raids and road blocks.

NCCL members observed the activity of the convoy and the police between 19th and 22nd June 1986, and attended during the eviction of travellers from Stoney Cross on 9 June 1986 and at various other times during May and June 1985 and 1986.

Farmer Attwell rightly received much public sympathy in his struggle to enforce his right to possession of land through the courts. His case raises the question of the lack of remedy available to those who are short of financial resources and legal expertise, whether the remedy is too slow and expensive, and why the police did not use their existing power under the law to assist Mr Attwell. Finally, the treatment of the convoy on its way to Stonehenge should not be separate from the lack of provision to others of a nomadic way of life.

This booklet is based on our observers' reports and press coverage in the media and reports of debates in Hansard. As we intend to produce this report to coincide with the Committee stage of the House of Lords debate on the Public Order Bill, we did not have the time to check the veracity of the many hearsay reports we received from travellers with the Convoy. Therefore we have not included them. Any report which chief constables may have given to their police authorities about the police operation over the solstice period has not been published, therefore we have included only the press reports of police statements and published letters, and police statements to ourselves. The civil liberties implications of the events surrounding the solstice at Stonehenge in 1985 and 1986 are set out below, as is the role of NCCL observers.

The events surrounding the attempt to hold a free festival at Stonehenge in June 1985 and 1986 raise varied and important civil liberty issues. These include a conflict between the civil liberties of the convoy to live in the way they wish and the social and economic right of farmers such as Mr Attwell to earn a living from the land.

The Caravan Sites Act 1968 attempted to solve such conflict between travelling and settled people by making provision for sites for travellers. This raises the question in respect of the convoy whether local authorities were under a duty to provide sites for these travellers. The official Department of Environment answer (see letter to NCCL, 27 June 1986, in appendix) is that there was no general duty but the local authority must examine whether individual members of the convoy are gypsies, i.e. of a nomadic habit of life who reguarly reside in or resort to a particular local authority area and therefore qualify for provision under the Caravan Sites Act. Many members of the convoy are of a nomadic way of life and regularly resort to Hampshire and Wiltshire. In this report we discuss their legal position in relation to the Caravan Sites Act.

If these travellers do come under the provision of the Caravan Sites Act, the question is raised as to whether there are already sufficient numbers of adequate sites provided for travellers, or if not, what powers can be used to obtain them.

Whether a site should be provided for a temporary festival at Stonehenge is a rather different issue. The question is raised as to whether government has the responsibility to provide a temporary site and, whether or not they have such a responsibility, whether they have a duty to do so to preserve the peace. Similarly the freedom of assembly is a hollow freedom unless one has somewhere to assemble. These different criteria are examined and we look at whether it is reasonable for national or local government to provide a site for a festival.

The background to the convoy is a 'moral panic' in which all travellers are identified as part of a unified whole, 'the convoy', and characterised as medieval brigands, carriers of AIDS or hepatitis. In this report we briefly examine some of these allegations. NCCL observers report that the backgrounds of the travellers in the convoy are as many and as varied as in an equivalent cross-section of settled people. Some travel with the convoy only at weekends or holidays, others have had a nomadic lifestyle for eight or more years. They are classed as 'hippies' but many are too young to have been part of the San Francisco generation. Some travellers have seasonal work, although there are complaints that this is now in short supply, others manufacture artefacts which they sell at local fairs. Some travellers claim social security, others do not. There is no evidence that a higher proportion of travellers with the convoy have criminal convictions than an equivalent cross-section of the settled community, as far as we know there have been no prosecutions for possession or distribution of hard drugs, nor have firearms been used, although one air rifle appears to have been found at Stoney Cross.

The extent of police public order powers and the way in which they are used to control the movements of the convoy cause NCCL great concern. We examine how extensive the existing powers are and whether in some cases they have been exceeded by the police. The Public Order Bill will give the police new powers over processions and assemblies and introduce a new offence of disorderly conduct. This report examines whether these new powers can be used in a discriminatory way against unpopular minorities and whether they will create rather than resolve conflict.

There has been a call for a new law of criminal trespass. We examine whether such a law is necessary or if it is desirable. The existing civil and criminal law in relation to trespass and its effects on freedom of movement as well as its effectiveness in providing a fast and effective remedy for private landowners is discussed.

Civil Liberties and the convoy

The National Council for Civil Liberties was founded in 1934 to defend civil and political rights such as freedom of speech and assembly. The need to establish an independent watchdog organisation resulted from the observation of police handling of the hunger marches in 1932.

In February 1934 Ronald Kidd, NCCL's first General Secretary, summoned to the Crypt of St Martin's in the Field Church 25 sympathisers – among them Harold Laski, Vera Brittain, Kingsley Martin, Edith Summerskill and Claud Cockburn – who joined the first executive committee and elected E M Forster as NCCL's first president. One week later the first 'vigilance committee' – independent observers charged with reporting on the behaviour of the hunger marchers and the police, gathered in Hyde Park at a meeting of unemployed workers, who, in the words of Kidd, were exercising the 'age-old liberty of the subject to demonstrate on an empty stomach'.

For the past 50 years NCCL, a non-party, non-denominational organisation, has continued to send independent observes to marches, demonstrations, pickets, public assemblies and public meetings. It has defended many charged with public order offences and has taken up test cases on important public order issues. Since its foundation NCCL's has had as its central concern the upholding of civil liberties as exemplified in the civil liberties charter shown at the end of this book. This argues that the right to peaceful assembly and peaceful protest should be upheld, that the limits of the criminal law should be applied fairly without discrimination against a group because of, for example, race, colour, appearance or life style and that every individual has a right to privacy. It is with these concerns at the forefront of our consideration that we set out here the reports of our observers who attended Stonehenge in June 1985 and June 1986, following the traditions of the vigilance committee of 1934. We are also aware of a conflict of civil liberties, for instance between travelling people and settled people, between Mr Attwell and the convoy, and produce this report in the hope of assisting to avoid similar conflicts in the future.

Factual Summary

The Background to the Stonehenge 'Free Festival'

The first free festival at Stonehenge was held in 1974 and has since been held annually up until 1984. Each festival lasted between one week and a month, which included the summer solstice on 21st June. Initially the police presence was low-key with little trouble, no arrests and only a daily tour of the site by two uniformed police officers. The numbers of people attending gradually rose to a peak of 30,000 in 1984. It became a festival feature that travellers living in vans, buses and trucks would leave the site in a convoy that moved on to the next free festival. Travelling by convoy gave a sense of safety and security. In 1982 the convoy moved onto Greenham Common Peace Camp and 'Peace Convoy' was stencilled on the side of some of the vehicles – a title that has persisted.

The 1985 Events

The build-up to the 1985 festival began early. In March, Wiltshire County Council, using the Road Traffic Regulation Act,* announced that between 13th May and 15th July the A344 around Stonehenge would be blocked off to traffic in certain areas. On 11th April the English Heritage, who are responsible for Stonehenge, the National Trust, who own 1,400 acres around it, and 17 co-plaintiffs applied for a 'precautionary injunction' against 83 named individuals said to represent the 'central element' of those likely to attend the festival. The National Trust began an advertising campaign in the music press and London's mainline and underground stations telling people that the festival would not take place that year.

In May, the Chief Constable of Wiltshire, Donald Smith, announced that he would have police on standby and additional help from neighbouring police forces to prevent the festival from taking place. Razor wire barricades were erected around the Stones. The police began to stop travellers moving through the west of England, warning them that if they proceeded towards Stonehenge they were in danger of causing a breach of the peace, which is an arrestable offence.

On 31st May, a convoy of 140 vehicles, escorted by the police, moved into Wiltshire and camped at Savernake Forest near Marlborough. Police, including a helicopter, surrounded the camp. On 1st June the convoy set off south down the A338 accompanied by the police, the helicopter, and the Earl of Cardigan, whose family owns Savernake Forest and leases it to the Forestry Commission. On arriving near Parkhouse the convoy was met by a police road block. Some members of the convoy tried to move away on the A303 to be confronted by another road block. The trapped convoy, surrounded by police, moved into an adjacent field. The police, in visored helmets, and carrying riot shields, followed and a pitched battle between the convoy and the police ensued. Moving away from the police, some convoy vehicles drove on to the next field which was planted with beans. The 'Battle of the

*For details of this provision, see *More Law, Less Order* below.

4

Beanfield' was well reported. The police followed each vehicle until it stopped or crashed. Television cameras saw the occupants of the vehicles, including children, being removed from what are their travelling homes. The Earl of Cardigan who witnessed the scene said:

'I shall never forget the screams of one woman who was holding up her little baby in a bus with smashed windows. She screamed and screamed at them to stop, but five seconds later 50 men with truncheons and shields just boiled into that bus. It was mayhem, no other word for it.'

Over 500 members of the convoy were arrested and charged with unlawful assembly, obstruction of the police and obstruction of the highway. The defendants appeared in court on 3rd June and the cases were adjourned until 31st July. A bail condition was imposed that they were not allowed to go within 25 miles of Stonehenge. Later the charge of unlawful assembly was dropped in all cases and the bail condition of 25 miles was reduced to a variety of distances from 7 to 15 miles. Most of the cases have still not been heard a year later, and in those that have, at least six defendants have been acquitted, with only a handful of convictions in contested cases. Fuller details of criminal cases arising from this incident are set out in the 'More Law, Less Order' section.

After the 'Battle of the Bean Field', the police impounded many of the convoy vehicles and took them to Everleigh. Further charges against some convoy members were preferred when people came to collect their vehicles.

Convoy members moved back to Savernake Forest, but a High Court eviction order granted to the Forestry Commission meant that they had to leave by 16th June. Approximately 100 travelling homes moved to Bratton Castle near Westbury and set up a camp.

Two other groups tried to reach Stonehenge in June. A group of 300 walked from Amesbury but were turned back by the police.

Also 35 'Pagans for Peace' walked from London accompanied by NCCL observers, so that they could celebrate births and marriages at dawn on 21st June and held their celebrations outside the Stones. A third group, the Druids, had agreed with the authorities not to go to the Stones.

In mid-June there were at least three police road checks set up between Savernake Forest and Stonehenge. People with long hair or 'convoy type' battered vehicles were observed by NCCL being stopped and turned back by the police, while other people committing traffic offences were not stopped. When stopping vehicles the police checked details on their radios, apparently with the police computer. They also ran through a questionnaire with each driver. The police stated that the checks had provided them with a great deal of 'intelligence'.

A second fence was erected around Stonehenge with extra guards and dogs and the English Heritage closed the monument to the public between 20th and 22nd June. On 18th June some members of the convoy applied, unsuccessfully, for an injunction barring the police and authorities from preventing people from going to Stonehenge. Although Mr Justice Steyn did not grant the injunction, he expressed concern that Special Action Security Force, was being used as a vigilante force to guard areas around Stonehenge.

The English Heritage and the Ministry of Defence, obtained a possession order against travellers camping at Bratton Castle. The Convoy left on 3rd July.

A Summary of Events Leading up to the June Solstice of 1986

FEBRUARY   Positions are taken up.
Thursday 6th   A group of Druids threaten to take Wiltshire County Council to the European Court of Human Rights if they are refused access to the Stones at the summer solstice.
Tuesday 25th   Wiltshire County Council records its formal opposition to an illegal free festival at Stonehenge in 1986.

MARCH   The church attempts to initiate compromise.
Friday 21st   The Reverend David Penney convened a large public meeting on behalf of the Diocesan Board for Social Responsibility at Salisbury City Hall to discuss how a solution to last year's impasse over the Festival could be found. No firm decisions reached.

APRIL   Festival campaigners try to negotiate. The authorities impose a ban.
Wednesday 9th   Wiltshire police, the National Trust and the English Heritage applied to the Chief Clerk of Wiltshire City Council to close part of the A344 between May 9th and June 30th.
Monday 28th   The Stonehenge '86 Campaign was launched. It: announced its intention to: –
(a) produce a regular magazine 'Festival Eye' to give news on negotiations over the festival;
(b) offer to shorten the Festival to 10-15 days;
(c) ask the National Trust to make an old airfield site near Stonehenge available for the festival;
(d) organise 'Stonehenge Freedom Marches'
(e) picket the English Heritage and National Trust Headquarters throughout May.
(f) picket Beaulieu Motor Museum, owned by Lord Montagu, the Chair of English Heritage in the first week of July.
(g) organise negotiating and co-ordinating meetings and lobby the House of Commons.
The English Heritage stated: 'In view of the threats of violence and demonstrations it is clearly impossible to give access to the Stones this year.'
MAY   Further preventative measures. Razor wire erected around Stonehenge; the Forestry Commission blocks all but one entrance to Savernake Forest with felled trees.
Thursday 1st   Stonehenge Free Festival supporters announced their

intention to hold a mass nude protest in Salisbury market square on 14th June.

Tuesday 13th   The English Heritage, Ministry of Defence, and 23 other landowners seek High Court injunction banning 49 named people from approaching within a four mile radius of Stonehenge. Adjournment sought by convoy.

Wednesday 14th   Festival organisers meet with senior Wiltshire police officers. The police state that anyone driving within five miles of the Stones will be stopped, pedestrians will be stopped within one mile of the Stones. They acknowledge that the Festival will carry on somewhere in this and future years. The police have now devised their contingency plans.

Friday 16th   Two High Court judges overturn a magistrates' decision to acquit members of the convoy arrested and charged with obstruction in 1985. Convoy vehicle passengers as well as the driver are held liable to be prosecuted for obstruction of the police where the driver stops and does not move from a police road block.

Saturday 17th   A convoy of 200 people converge on the Stones, surprising everyone. 380 police move the convoy off the site. No violence, no arrests.

Meeting held at Salisbury Town Hall; a compromise over the Festival sought. National Trust and English Heritage confirm that there is no possibility of a Festival.

Sunday 18th   Convoy moves to Camel Hill near Sparkford, supervised by police officers.

Tuesday 20th   English Heritage, Ministry of Defence and landowners injunction granted.

Thursday 22nd   Wiltshire police launch 'Operation Solstice' and state that a festival would be a 'serious threat to law and order'. Chief Constable Donald Smith described the convoy as 'very vicious people to deal with'.

Friday 23rd   Convoy ejected from Camel Hill and move two miles to Mr Attwell's farm at Lytes Cary. 100 vehicles, 300 people and a herd of goats camp there, ruining Mr Attwell's grass crop for silage.

Monday 26th   National Farmers' Union expressed outrage at the fact that in cases of trespass on private land it is the landowner who is responsible for applying to the court for an eviction order, a process which takes up to five days. The landowner can risk using 'reasonable force' to remove trespassers but he or she cannot gain police assistance to evict until the court order has been granted. The NFU urges the givernment to find a permanent site for the festival on Ministry of Defence land and secondly urges that trespass on private land should be made a criminal rather than a civil offence (see *More Law, Less Order* below).

Tuesday 27th   Minister of State for Agriculture, Mr John Selwyn Gummer, visits the convoy at Mr Attwell's farm. Calls the convoy 'common criminals'.

Thursday 29th   100 people from the convoy drive to Yeovil to collect unemployment and supplementary benefit. The DHSS draft in more staff to deal with claims.

Mr David Mellor, Home Office Minister, interviewed on BBC radio responds to pressure for legal remedy to the convoy's actions. Explains that the forthcoming Public Order Bill will make cases of disorderly conduct on private land a criminal offence, but not those of trespass.

He states that there is no need for a criminal trespass offence, that there is a danger that innocent persons would fall foul of such a criminal offence and that the Public Order Bill is not the appropriate legislation to contain such an offence.

Mr Humphrey Temperley, Chair of Somerset's Planning Committee says that 'the government are not doing their job to provide a framework' to enable each county to set up proper travellers' sites so that people like the convoy wouldn't have reason to squat on private land.

High Court eviction order granted to Mr Attwell. *Today* newspaper offer to pay the £5,000 legal costs.

Another group, Rainbow Village, set up at Lyng near Mr Attwell's farm on a disused stretch of road. Say they have been moved 35 times in two years.

Friday 30th Convoy agree to leave Mr Attwell's farm peacefully. Neighbouring farmers block off and guard all entrances to their land with farm machinery, piles of manure, some armed with staves, one farmer with a double-barrelled shot-gun.

Mr Robert Boscawan, Conservative MP for Somerset and Frome, visits Mr Attwell's farm. Convoy children throw mud at him.

Convoy moves off towards Dorset, their progress monitored by police, a police helicopter and farmers with CB radios. Late at night, at the county border, 15 police vehicles and 300 police in riot gear, protective headgear and capes without identifying numbers, stop the convoy on the A37 at Melbury Osmond. Police check convoy members for criminal records, check vehicles and tell the convoy that they cannot move because they might cause a breach of the peace.

Paddy Ashdown, Liberal MP for Yeovil, tries to negotiate between convoy and police. At the front of the three-mile-long convoy are Dorset Police; at the rear are the Avon and Somerset force. Police state they are preventing a breach of the peace occurring. Some convoy members arrested and later released without charge. Eventually Paddy Ashdown agrees with police that convoy should move off in five groups. Convoy wants to stay reasonably close together as fear attack on them by local farmers, police fear the same.

Country Landowners' Association calls for:
(a) Speedier eviction machinery for farmers and landowners when mass invasions of their property occur;
(b) Amendments to Public Order Bill to enable police to deal with trespass on private land.

Saturday 31st   At 3.30am the police escort the convoy towards Corfe Castle in Dorset. Helicopter flies above convoy. The police keep the convoy moving but occasionally convoy vehicles break down. They reach Corfe Castle and spend the night in a by-road (B3351) to which police have directed them. Paddy Ashdown tells the press that he cannot understand Dorset police actions and that he was not sure that the police have the legal power to stop the convoy on the main highway. Clive Soley, Labour MP and spokesman on Home Affairs, accuses the government of using the police as 'a private army'.

JUNE   The convoy becomes a law and order issue

Sunday 1st   Police escort the convoy onto the A351, and warn them that they must keep moving and anyone who stops would face possible arrest. Approximately 400 adults and 100 children on the convoy. *The Guardian* reports that two convoy vehicles which did not obey police instructions were ramed by police Transit vans. Convoy moves onto A31 and is herded back northwards to the Hampshire border. Convoy arrives at Stoney Cross, a disused Second World War airfield in the New Forest owned by the Crown Estate Commission. Convoy stop on roadside verge. The Chief Constable of Hampshire, John Duke, has a message announced by the police helicopter to say that the convoy is obstructing the highway and must move by 3.30pm or face arrest. The convoy has been on the road for ten hours; some vehicles require repairs and fuel. The convoy moves off the highway.

A group of 30-40 people begin walking from London to Salisbury to make a nude protest there on 14th June.

Monday 2nd   Mr Baker, MP for Dorset North, Mr Ward, MP for Poole and Mr McNair-Wilson, MP for the New Forest, visit Stoney Cross. MPs call for tougher provisions in the Public Order Bill and restrictions on convoy members drawing social security. John Duke, Hampshire's Chief Constable, visits Stoney Cross and asks the convoy to leave. He is barracked and jeered. Mr Duke denies that the police had any responsibility for bringing the convoy to the Forest. He talks of 'neutralising this invasion'. Mr Duke said the convoy faced arrest for obstruction if they did not move.

150 'ordinary' campers evacuated from the Forest because of 'health risk'.

Man jailed for 30 days by Poole Magistrates' Court for ramming a police vehicle with his Austin hearse. Could not pay fine of £520. He alleges that the windows of the hearse had been smashed by police truncheons, before the ramming incident.

Chair of the new Forest Association calls for an offence to be created where a vehicle travels more than 20 feet on to private land without the landowners' permission.

Tuesday 3rd   Ministry of Agriculture lawyers applied for possession order against convoy in the New Forest. The NCCL spoke to the Director General of the Forestry Commission, Mr Holmes, by telephone and asked him not to proceed with the eviction. Mr Holmes said:

1] Stoney Cross is valuable heritage land.

2] He feared that the longer the convoy were allowed to stay on the land the more difficult it would become to remove them.

3] He feared that the convoy would see the Forestry Commission as a 'soft touch' if they did not proceed with the eviction.

He said that for these reasons the Forestry Commission would be obtaining an injunction within the next few days.

All cars leaving Stoney Cross are checked by police. An NCCL observer noted that people failing to give a permanent address were threatened with arrest.

In the House of Commons Mr Hurd, Home Secretary, describes the convoy as 'a band of medieval brigands who have no respect for the law or the rights of others.' Mr Soley, Labour spokesman on Home Affairs, accuses members of the Conservative Party 'when they talk of making people conform, that is precisely the language that was used in Nazi Germany, and that when people failed to conform they were put in concentration camps and gas chambers.'

The Lord Chancellor's Department examines how the eviction process for farmers and private landowners can be speeded up. Wiltshire police have drafted in a surveillance vehicle from the Home Office with infra red video camera and riot screens front and rear to watch over the convoy.

DHSS states that it has officers travelling where the convoy goes and that this scheme was launched in 1985.

Mr Hurd states intention to tighten up laws on the roadworthiness of vehicles.

Wednesday 4th   Trustees of the Longford estate successfully apply for a possession order to prevent convoy members from camping on the estate.

Thursday 5th   Ministry of Agriculture obtains High Court hearing for possession order for Stoney Cross camp. Roy Hughes for the Forestry Commission gives reasons for eviction as:
(a) fear that more would join the camp;
(b) sanitation facilities inadequate for 300;
(c) fear that a festival would be held on the site;
(d) fear of a threat to public order.

The judge grants the eviction order and asks the Minister for Agriculture, Mr Jopling, to 'stay his hand for seven days' to allow an orderly and gradual dispersal of the convoy. Convoy interprets judgement as a seven-day reprieve.

Convoy members go to Tatton to claim social security to cover cost of food, repairs and fuel.

Country Landowners' Association urges that publicly funded compensation be paid where the convoy trespassed on private land.

The Gypsy Council calls for a 'cooling off' period.

Police arrest ten convoy members for motoring offences. Four are released after questioning.

In the House of Commons, Mrs Thatcher expresses her personal dislike of the convoy and says 'if the present law is inadequate, we will have to introduce fresh law' to deal with the convoy. Mrs Thatcher states she will set up a ministerial committee to investigate wide-ranging changes to the law of trespass. She also says that she is 'only too delighted to do anything we can to make life difficult for such things as hippy convoys'. It is reported that the Cabinet spent almost half of its meeting discussing the hippy convoy.

Flock of sheep savaged by two dogs allegedly owned by the convoy.

Judge who granted eviction order on Stoney Cross calls a press conference. Explains his judgement as directing that the convoy should start moving off the Stoney Cross camp immediately. If the camp did not do so he expected that the Forestry Commission would enforce the eviction before the seven days were up.

Friday 6th   A confidential DHSS report of the Nomadic Claimant's Working Party is leaked to the press. Its recommendations included the following:

(a) a national register of social security claims by the convoy should be kept to prevent fraud and curb payments;

(b) installation of protective screens in DHSS offices where there were convoy claimants;

(c) stricter checks to be introduced so that convoy members would have to 'prove' parentage of children for who they claimed;

(d) officers to avoid visiting convoy camps as it would be 'potentially dangerous';

(e) information on convoys to be put on a national computer;

(f) restriction of urgent needs payments because their communal life-style meant that convoy members could borrow from one another.

The report stated that some convoy members have hepatitis. The report was criticised by the civil service unions and Labour MPs. Also that the recommendations would break rules of confidentiality.

Saturday 7th   Government spokesperson for the Environment, Lord Davidson, is reported as saying that there were strong arguments against making trespass a criminal offence, as it would apply to ramblers who strayed from footpaths.

Strict security cordon around Stoney Cross camp.

Convoy reported as saying they did not want to stage a festival in the New Forest.

Also reported as being afraid to leave camp, fearing arrest by police.

Monday 9th   Police 'Operation Daybreak'. Police evict convoy from Stoney Cross at dawn. 129 vehicles impounded, 64 convoy members are arrested. 440 police encircled camp, no resistance put up by the convoy. All approach roads sealed and police clear camp in two hours. Police from Hampshire, Dorset, Wiltshire, Avon and Somerset. Police carried files on all vehicles, and vehicles are impounded where declared unroadworthy.

250 convoy members left the camp by foot on the A31 in a light drizzle of rain. Hampshire Social Services provided a coach to take people to an emergency reception centre at an old aircraft hangar in Calshot. Some convoy members boarded coach but most walked along the road. More convoy walkers took a ride on the coach after a further five mile trek.

At Calshot convoy members were given food, accommodation and travel warrants. 70 convoy members took the train to Bristol intending to go on to the Glastonbury CND festival site by bus.

Special magistrates' court set up in Southampton. The defendants arrested earlier that day are charged with obstruction, threatening behaviour and possession of drugs. In all cases heard then, defendants were either fined, given a conditional discharge, or bound over to keep the peace.

70 walkers continued to walk for 14 hours toward the CND festival site. Spent night at Horton where a farmer agreed they could stay.

Tuesday 10th   Convoy members stay the night at Zig Zag Hill near Shaftesbury, Dorset.

Thursday 12th   Another group of convoy campers at Worthy Farm, Pilton, the CND festival site, evicted by farm owner Michael Eavis. Mr Eavis says he was forced to evict to safeguard the festival. He says that his neighbours were angry at the presence of the convoy and that his insurance cover for the festival has been withdrawn while the convoy remains on site.

Local grazers' association take court action to evict a travelling group from land on the Black Mountain in Wales where they had stayed for four years.

The Common Land Forum urge that common land should be open to the public as of right which is not the case with rural commons at present.

Police reinforcements are sent to Wincanton where 100 convoy members are making their way to Glastonbury.

Saturday 14th   Wiltshire County Council are granted an order under the 1847 Town Police Clauses Act to forbid processions from entering Salisbury on the 14th and 15th June. The would-be nude protesters are therefore restricted to moving around Salisbury ringroad accompanied by the police, before moving off to Grovely Woods.

Sunday 15th   It is reported that some of a 500-700 convoy members, including people who have walked from London, camp at Yarnbury Castle hill fort. The convoy includes 60-100 vehicles which are reported as being a well-ordered column of roadworthy and taxed cars and vans. Others in the convoy travel to Hanging Langford.

Wednesday 18th   A letter from the Chief Constable of Wiltshire, Donald Smith, (see Appendix II) sets out the conditions under which 300 people can conduct peaceful ceremonies at Stonehenge on the solstice. Six conditions are laid down including the necessity of the visitors travelling by hired coach, and that groups of up to 100 can carry out ceremonies for up to one hour each.

Friday 20th   More than 200 convoy members with 80 vehicles who have been encamped at Hanging Langford prepare to move off in obedience to an injunction. Under the supervision of the police, they emerge onto the A36 and are directed to the west in the direction of Warminster, i.e. away from Stonehenge. A short distance further on the road becomes a dual carriageway. On it a massive police roadblock has

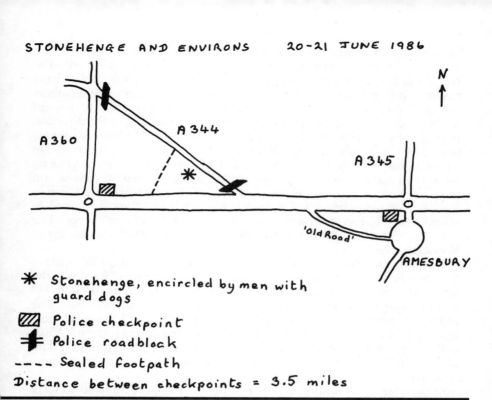

STONEHENGE AND ENVIRONS   20-21 JUNE 1986

A360

A344

A345

'Old Road'

AMESBURY

N ↑

✳ Stonehenge, encircled by men with guard dogs

▨ Police checkpoint

⧯ Police roadblock

---- Sealed footpath

Distance between checkpoints = 3.5 miles

A36. WESTBOUND SECTION OF DUAL CARRIAGEWAY BETWEEN WILTON AND WARMINSTER - 20 JUNE 1986

← Warminster   Wilton →

Central reservation, on which 22 police vehicles, mostly Transit vans, are parked

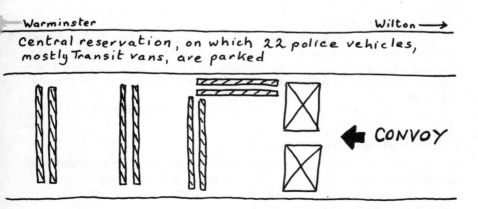

← CONVOY

▨▨▨▨ Line of police officers (approx. 300 on area shown)

⊠ Police Range Rover

13

been set up. It comprises some 300 police from Wiltshire and six other authorities together with approximately 24 vehicles (see diagram). The convoy is forced to halt. After an hour, during which more police have assembled to the rear, the officers at the front instruct convoy members to leave their vehicles and move back along the road, i.e. toward Stonehenge. This they do peacefully and, while walking in the direction indicated by the police, are arrested for obstruction. The vehicle owners who left their vehicles, many of which are also their homes, are subsequently charged with obstruction of the highway by a vehicle. More than 200 people are arrested. NCCL observers see no violence on the part of either convoy members or police. Those arrested are taken to the police headquarters at Devizes from which most are dispersed to spend the night in custody. A few are released without charge. The vehicles and other property are removed, as last year, to the tip at Everleigh which does service as a vehicle pound.

That evening, NCCL observers note police checkpoints on the A303 at the roundabouts to each side of Stonehenge. (See map.) The A344, the approach road to Stonehenge, which is closed by injunction, has a roadblock at either end where it meets the A303 and the A360. The public footpath past Stonehenge between the A303 and the A344, also subject to a closure order, is sealed. At the checkpoints on the A303, police officers request name, address, vehicle registration number, date of birth, place of birth, occupation, height and eye colour from some road users.

Saturday 21st   A limited number of people (200) are allowed to walk along the A344 to the area adjacent to the Stones for the solstice. These include druids, secular druids, some local people, the press and about 100 hippies. There are about 100 police between the gathering and Stonehenge itself. More police with dogs surround the Stones and helicopters circle overhead. At 6 a.m. the police move people away and the road is again closed.

Magistrates' Courts are set up in Salisbury and Swindon. In Salisbury, prisoners are brought to court handcuffed. In both courts defendants are charged with obstruction of the highway and of the police. All cases are adjourned with bail conditions that include exclusion from the County of Wiltshire.

Some of the convoy move on to Kings' Somborne in Hampshire.

Information and Misinformation

During 1985 and 1986 there were many accusations made about the activities of the convoy and the police, pursuing their respective aims of trying to organise a festival and trying to prevent one. In this section some of the allegations are examined.

1. The terms of the 1985 injunction and police powers

In the report of Her Majesty's Chief Inspector of Constabulary 1985, it is stated 'a violent confrontation took place at Parkhouse in Wiltshire on

Saturday 1st June when a convoy of 170 vehicles was being driven toward Stonehenge at the time of the summer solstice celebrations, in clear defiance of injunctions which were in force'.

In April 1985 the English Heritage, and National Trust, took out a 'precautionary injunction' against 50 named people said to represent the 'central element' of those likely to attend the festival.

It is not a police responsibility to enforce an injunction. In any case the injunction only referred to those named individuals and did not refer to all convoy travellers in the way in which it was enforced by the police.

2. Damage to the Stones

Mrs T M Stevenson of the Home Office in a letter to Dr M C Stevenson dated 1st August 1985 stated that 'the risk involved and the damage occurring (to the Stones) had become unacceptably high' for a festival to be held on the site.

The English Heritage have a duty to protect the Stones but accounts of damage are contradictory.

The Guardian commented in an article on 24th June 1985 that, 'The Ministry of Defence has done damage to monuments of similar construction and probably more importance, all over Salisbury Plain.'

3. Ramming or Rammed against?

On 9th June Mr Duke, Chief Constable of Hampshire was quoted as saying that the convoy contained:

'a self-styled potentially violent group called The Warriors which, in the past have been prepared to use their vehicle as battering rams.'

No further evidence of The Warrior group was recorded, but *The Guardian* had reported on 2nd of June that as the convoy moved from Corfe Castle there was

'The near destruction of a police vehicle in one of two incidents in which police cars rammed convoy vehicles.'

4. Devilish or disaffected?

On 3rd June Mr Hurd, the Home Secretary, described the convoy as:

'a band of medieval brigands who have no respect for law and order and the rights of others'.

This assertion was made without any evidence being presented that the convoy contained a higher proportion of people with criminal records or evidence that the travellers were committing offences on the road.

A letter to *The Guardian* published on 6th June described how a couple who were sightseeing at Stonehenge decided to see the convoy for themselves. They reported that:

'Many of those to whom we spoke had held down jobs and paid rates and taxes like "normal" peole, but had been made redundant several times . . . they feel disaffected and have sought an alternative way of life.'

5. Even-handed law enforcement?

On 20th June at Hanging Langford, the Wiltshire Police press officer told an NCCL observer that the convoy would be 'treated like any other road user'.

The *Bournemouth Evening Echo*, in its editorial on 2nd June had already commented on the way in which farmers were not arrested for blocking roads but the convoy was.

'We would also like to hear a legal definition of the stage when blocking a road ceases to be causing obstruction – because what emerges in the present situation is one law for the farmers and one for the travellers, both of whom, in the circumstances are operating off their private property'.

6. Vicious or Not?

On 22nd June Chief Constable Donald Smith of the Wiltshire force said:

'The convoy is a group of people who have no respect for law and order. They are very vicious people to deal with in any situation, they are vagrants.'

There was little evidence that the convoy had acted provocatively. They had not resisted eviction at Hanging Langford or Stoney Cross.

Such statements resulted in people living locally to the convoy's path being very worried. Cllr. and Mrs Duffy live on the road where the convoy were made to camp on 31st May. Mrs Duffy was reported as saying that she kept an all-night vigil:

'I've not had a wink of sleep, but they are quiet enough and we've had no real trouble.'

7. Disperse them or give them a site?

Mr Baker, MP for Dorset North in the House of Commons on 3rd June stated that:

'the problem of such a convoy which consists of 130 vehicles, derives from its size. Therefore policies designed to disperse such a convoy and to include a provision in the Public Order Bill which will allow us to deal with large mass convoys of this kind is the correct approach.'

On 29th May Mr Temperley, Chair of Somerset's Planning Committee had stated:

'It is clear to me . . . that the problem is not going to go away. Nor do I believe that it is going to be solved by the approach of shoot them, gas them and send them back to the cities where they came from.

What I am unhappy about is that when presented with a problem which is clearly growing and which we predicted a year ago, the government are not doing their job to provide a framework on which we can make decisions.'

He also stated:

'I can't justify spending our ratepayers' money providing a site if I don't have a duty to do so.'

8. Unsubstantiated allegations

There have also been a number of adverse comments made about the convoy.

MP for Salisbury, Robert Key, warned that there was an 'explosion of hepatitis and AIDS' associated with the 'evil' festival.

On 17th April the *Salisbury Journal* printed a letter from John Sarum, Bishop of Salisbury, who alleged that 'children were heavily at risk, for example from fire accidents, because of neglect by those supposedly in charge of them'.

In neither of these cases were the allegations supported by any evidence.

9. Arms and the convoy or farmer

Mr Duke, Chief Constable of Hampshire, reported that after the eviction of the convoy from Stoney Cross the police found 'a high velocity rifle equipped with a telescopic sight' in an abandoned vehicle. It was later confirmed that the gun was an air rifle.

The *Daily Telegraph* reported on 31st May 1986 that one young man with the farmers had with him a double-barrelled shotgun and that a farmer stated that he would shoot the convoy rather than have them on his land.

No Trespassers

In May 1986, the civil law of trespasss was effectively used by landowners to exclude almost 50 potential trespassers from a five mile zone around Stonehenge. In contrast Farmer Attwell complained that the law failed to provide a fast and effective method of ousting actual trespassers from his land.

Although David Mellor, interviewed by BBC radio in early June stated that there was not a need to change criminal trespass law, on 29th June 1986, the *Sunday Times* reported that the Home Secretary intended to 'make trespass on private land by hippy convoys a criminal offence'. In this section we examine the existing law of trespass, its use in relation to the convoy, whether the change in the law is necessary to protect the rights of landowners to exclusive occupation of their land and the effect that such a change may have.

Background

No previous government has considered legislating for a full law of criminal trespass. In 1974 the Law Commission (Working Paper No. 54) proposed two criminal offences of entering and remaining on property, despite the fact that the then government had decided 'not to create at this stage an offence of criminal trespass'. This proposal, arising out of complaints about squatters, was enacted in a modified form in the Criminal Law Act 1977. But these offences dealt principally with residential premises; they did not cover the adverse occupation of open land. A Private Member's Bill put forward by the Earl of Onslow in 1984 was similarly limited. It passed through the House of Lords but failed to complete its stages in the House of Commons through lack of support and the efforts of the 'homelessness' lobby.

Otherwise, unwanted occupiers of fields would normally be ejected by the civil law procedures (see below) or by the police arresting those who had committed criminal offences such as damage to crops or by self-help by the owner, sometimes with the help of the police where a breach of the peace was anticipated (see below).

An attempt by the Country Landowners' Association to extend to private land the proposed police powers under the Public Order Bill to limit numbers, duration and location of assemblies to public land was defeated after vigorous lobbying by mountaineers, ramblers and civil libertarians, and government opposition.

In early June 1986 the Minister of State at the Home Office David Mellor was still maintaining the position that there was no need for a law of criminal trespass, that a criminal trespass offence would create more problems, particularly for innocent ramblers or visitors to property, than it would solve, that the Public Order Bill gave the police sufficient powers to act to remove wrong-doers, and that the Public Order Bill was not the right place for a new law of criminal trespass anyway.

A civil offence relates to behaviour in public between two private individuals, and a criminal offence relates to behaviour which offends against the public or the state. The police cannot act on a civil offence until and unless the court has agreed they can.

But in late June 1986 (*The Times*, 24th June 1986) the Attorney-General informed the House of Commons that (a) the Home Secretary was considering strengthening police powers under the Public Order Bill or creating a limited form of criminal trespass, and (b) the Lord Chancellor was considering improvements to the civil procedure for the summary repossession of land. The Attorney-General made it clear that the government retained reservations about a criminal trespass offence and the sort of cases which, in his view, should never be made criminal offences.

The Law

Meaning of Trespass

A person commits trespass to land if he or she intentionally, negligently or recklessly enters or remains on land in the possession of another. It is trespass to go on the land or to put or leave anything (including vehicles) on the land. Not all forms of entry on to private land amount to a trespass, for example a postman can have implied permission to enter. However in law a squatter is a trespasser. He or she has no interest in the house or land occupied which would enable him or her to defend possession proceedings brought against him/her by the owner or person entitled to occupation. Contrary to popular belief, a squatter is not committing a crime merely by entering on open land, although other criminal offences may follow (see below). If the owner-occupier wishes to eject him or her, the owner-occupier should take civil proceedings through the courts.

The Owner-Occupier's Remedies in relation to trespass on open land

(i)   The possessor of land, usually the owner or tenant, can sue the trespasser for the return of the possession of land at any time. This is the most effective way of removing trespassers from open land. After a trespasser has been asked to leave and refuses and an order for possession has been granted and served on the trespassers, *either* (a) the trespassers can be forcibly ejected by the Sheriff in High Court proceedings or by the Bailiffs in County Court proceedings – the police are enpowered to assist the Sheriff but not the Bailiff – *or* (b) the possessor can take contempt of court proceedings against trespassers which could lead ultimately to imprisonment.

Following the Department of the Environment's 'Consultative Paper on Squatting' (August 1975) special rules of court* were drafted to provide a speedy and effective procedure to reclaim land and to evict trespassers. Proceedings can be served on named defendants or, where it is not reasonably practicable to identify the trespassers or unnamed persons by fixing copies of the document to the main door or 'other conspicuous part of the premises'. This procedure is designed to operate without a trial with witnesses, although defendants with a genuine claim will be entitled to a full trial of the action. An order for possession will not normally be made for five days, but the period may be shorter in case of urgency. There is no power to suspend the order for possession unless the owner consents.

(ii)   The possessor of land can sue the trespasser for compensation if any loss or damage has been caused.

(iii)   The possessor of land can sue the trespasser for an injunction restraining the trespasser from continuing or repeating the trespass.

(iv)   The possessor can exercise his or her common law right of re-entry and use reasonable force to eject the trespasser, although this course is not advisable in view of the risk of injury or damage to property in the process of the Criminal Law Act 1977. In any event a trespasser who has entered without force should also be requested to leave first.

*Order 113 in the High Court, Order 24 in the County Court

(v)   The possessor can call in the police when any criminal offence has been committed.

The Criminal Law

There is no comprehensive criminal law of trespass. The familiar notice 'trespassers will be prosecuted' is an empty threat. It is not a crime to walk across someone else's land without permission, or to refuse to leave having been told to do so.

There are however a number of limited offences (crimes) of criminal trespass. They are intended principally to protect premises from squatters, although in the main they are cumbersome charges and the police prefer to use either the offences contrary to Sections 1 and 3 of the Criminal Damage Act 1971 of criminal damage or of possessing anything with intent to damage property.

The existing offences of criminal trespasses are as follows:

Violence for securing entry;

Adverse occupation of residential premises;

Trespassing with an offensive weapon;

Trespassing on premises of foreign missions;

Burglary (which involves the person entering the building as trespasser)

The police are empowered to act against trespassers:

(a)   To make an arrest for one of the offences above or for the offence of resisting or intentionally obstructing on officer of the court, such as the Sheriff enforcing possession proceedings.

(b)   To make an arrest for any other offence committed on the land or premises, for example, criminal damage, assault (including attempts or threats to commit damage or to assault).

(c)   To detain or disperse using police preventative powers where a breach of the peace is being committed (for example by trespassers resisting a farmer's attempts to evict them from his land), or where it is reasonably believed that a breach of the peace is imminent, or where a breach of the peace has been committed and it is reasonably believed that a renewal of it is threatened and, if necessary, to take that person before a Magistrates' Court to be bound over.

The Case of Farmer Attwell and the Law of Trespass

In May 1986, approximately 300 'itinerant hippies' (see *The Times* 31st May 1986) occupied land belonging to a Somerset farmer. At the end of a week, the trespassers were evicted by Sheriff's officers under the civil procedure for possession set out above. Some Members of Parliament claimed that the case demonstrated the need for a law of criminal trespass, to make it a criminal offence to enter land (open land or buildings) as a trespasser or to remain on land as a trespasser after being required to leave. The police, it was said, had been powerless to act.

But the delay in evicting the trespassers may not have been the fault of the law –

(a)   Summary procedure in the High Court (and to a lesser extent in the County Court) is normally speedy and effective once put into motion, and possession orders can be obtained from the duty judge at weekends and out of court hours. In cases of urgency – and Mr Attwell claimed that damage was being caused to his property which would make it an urgent case – the normal five-day period can be waived. It seems that Mr Attwell had two problems. First he lacked funds to bring proceedings. The strict means test may have prevented his obtaining legal aid (eventually the newspaper *Today* paid his legal fees). Secondly, there was some delay in the procedure in the proceedings at the local court.

(b)   In any event the police were not powerless to act. If criminal offences had been committed, such as criminal damage, the police were entitled, in fact had a duty, to enter the land and arrest those responsible or at least attempt to find out who was responsible. If it was impossible to identify the culprits, the police were entitled to use their preventative powers to prevent a breach of the peace, which was certainly imminent in view of the behaviour of local residents who were threatening to use shotguns. By this means the police could have moved on the trespassers and if they had refused to comply with the police instructions to move on, arrested them (if the general arrest conditions of Section 25, Police and Criminal Evidence Act 1984, applied*) for obstructing the police in the execution of their duty or for any other criminal offence committed (for example, assault or threatening, abusive or insulting words or behaviour, under Section 5 Public Order Act 1936). Why the police did not act is uncertain. Some have suggested that they still had many cases outstanding from the year before. But it is more likely that the police were displaying a reluctance to become involved in anything to do with the civil law (a common complaint of those involved in domestic disputes, particularly of women in domestic violence cases).

The Case of 25 Landowners, the Peace Convoy and the Law of Trespass

In May 1986 an application was made to the High Court by 25 local landowners for an injunction preventing approximately 50 named

---

*General arrest conditions are: 1 the police officer does not know what the suspect's name and cannot readily find out what it is; 2 the police officer believes the name given is false; 3 the suspect has failed to give an address which the police believe he/she will be at long enough to be served with a summons or someone else will be at who could receive the summons; 4 the police officer believes that arrest is necessary to prevent the person: a causing injury to him/herself or someone else; b suffering injury; c causing loss or damage to property; d committing an offence against public decency; e causing an unlawful obstruction of the highway. 5 the police officer believes that arrest is necessary to protect a child or other vulnerable person.

persons from entering their land. The landowners included the National Trust and English Heritage who are responsible for the Stonehenge monument. All the plaintiffs owned land within five miles of Stonehenge. The defendants were chosen on the basis of information provided by the Wiltshire Police. The Wiltshire Police assisted the application, and a police officer from the 'Stonehenge Intelligence Unit' stated that the main defendants were all involved in the organisation of the festival. Four defendants appeared at the hearing. The judge, while granting the injunction, refused it in respect of three individuals against whom he considered he had no evidence that they intended to trespass. This effectively created what was to be called an 'exclusion zone' around Stonehenge. The police set up road blocks around the area on the grounds that there was 'imminent danger of breach of the police' (but see 'More Law, Less Order' below) and NCCL observers saw several people being turned back from the area, who were not of the 50 named (see 'Factual Summary' above). From the point of view of the 25 landowners the law of trespass had provided a very effective preventative power for them to exclude travellers from their land around the solstice. Physical barriers, farm machinery etc, were also placed across access to land around the monument.

Conclusion

It is clear from the contrasting experiences of Farmer Attwell and the 25 landowners that the single litigant of limited means may be at a disadvantage when attempting to enforce the law of trespass. However · this is clearly an argument for expanding legal aid rather than bypassing the civil courts to give the police powers to step in. The summary procedure for trespassers can be rapid and the police have powers to prevent a wide range of criminal offences from criminal damage to breach of the peace.

Both forms of a criminal trespass law presently being mooted have grave drawbacks. The Ramblers' Association, the British Mountaineering Society and various other recreational groups pointed out that the Country Landowners amendment to the Public Order Bill would catch groups of walkers, birdwatchers and climbers straying on to private land. In some circumstances walkers may be reclaiming what they believe to be common land, or traditional rights of way. In these circumstances it is not appropriate to give the police public order powers to intervene in complex questions of ownership and rights of access. A representative from the National Farmers' Union in a radio broadcast in June 1986, seemed to favour an offence of failing to leave land which one has entered as a trespasser after a warning has been given. However, although this would exclude groups who inadvertently wandered on to private land, it still has serious defects. It would give the police a duty to intervene in complex questions of civil law relating to ownership of land, particularly neighbour disputes over boundaries, for example if it were a criminal offence a police constable would be put in the difficult position of trying to sort out the ownership of the land. It may place complex legal decisions over title and right of way in the hands of the criminal courts rather than the civil courts which are more suited to deal with these disputes; and it may turn what amounts to a civil wrong into a criminal offence although no damage or injury has been caused.

More Law, Less Order

Both local and national government neglected to do their duty to provide a site for travellers on their way to Stonehenge for the solstice (though they do not have a duty to provide a festival site). They relied upon the police, using a wide range of public order powers, to deal with the problems that may arise from travellers arriving in the area where no additional sites have been provided. A panoply of public order powers, ranging from powers to prevent breach of the peace, to enforcement of road closure orders, to the use of the Road Traffic Act, were stretched to their limits to exclude, contain and, in the words of the Chief Constable of Hampshire, to 'neutralise' the travellers. NCCL observers noted on several occasions, (for example, the stopping of cars containing long-haired 'hippy' type people near Stonehenge in June 1985, while cars committing moving traffic offences were not intercepted). Police powers were used in a manner which discriminated against people who appeared to be members of the convoy.

In this section we look at the powers used by the police, the role of the courts in failing to set clear limits to these powers, and the role of the Inspector of Constabulary in examining the operational decisions which led to the 'Battle of the Beanfield' in June 1985. The police operation also raises questions of privacy in relation to the information collected from travellers and other users of the highway over the solstice period in 1985 and 1986.

Rather than codifying wide and vague police powers, the Public Order Bill presently before Parliament introduces both more police public order powers and more discretion. We examine how the Bill's powers could be implemented in 1987 if it were passed in its present form.

Freedom of movement

There is no right of assembly in English law, only the right to pass and re-pass along the highway without let or hindrance. Restrictions have been placed on the travellers' freedom of movement in six particular ways. First, the police have used roadblocks to divert the convoy. The legality of this tactic is questionable since the only justification is to prevent a breach of the peace, and the somewhat bedraggled travellers have, in the main, been extremely peaceful. Secondly, road checks have been set up, for example around the camp, where travellers on foot and in vehicles were stopped, questioned and generally allowed to proceed in or out of the camp. The Police and Criminal Evidence Act 1984 gives the police specific powers to stop and search both vehicles and pedestrians for both stolen goods, firearms, drugs and offensive weapons but this did not apply to these stops. Thirdly, a general order was made under Section 21 of the Town Police Clauses Act 1847 by Salisbury District Council in June 1986 banning 'hippies' from the city centre for two specified days to prevent a protest march taking place. Fourthly, a road closure order was made in relation to the A344 leading to Stonehenge, by Wiltshire Council. Fifthly, some 230 travellers were arrested for obstruction of the highway at Hanging Langford on Friday 20 June 1986. Finally, wide ranging bail conditions were imposed by Salisbury and Wiltshire magistrates on over 200 travellers, requiring them to leave the County of Wiltshire by midnight.

1. Roadblocks

There is no general power vested in the police either at common law or by statute to create road blocks. The Police and Criminal Evidence Act 1984 provides a power to set up roadblocks for vehicles, but the power is limited mainly to the search for suspects and witnesses of crimes. This does not apply to the situation in Wiltshire and Hampshire preceding the solstice.

However, courts have held that a police constable has the power to stop and turn back motor vehicles if she or he has reasonable grounds for believing that a breach of the peace is imminent. In *Moss v. Mclachlan*, a case generally considered to turn on its particular facts, striking miners were turned back two miles from a colliery where there had earlier been disorder and five miles from another. The Divisional Court emphasised that the possibility of a breach of the peace must be real, imminent and immediate, in the sense that it was in close proximity both in place and time, to justify any preventative action.

This action, sometimes known as the 'intercept policy' was widely used in Nottinghamshire during the miners' dispute. Those who disobeyed or queried the instructions were arrested for obstructing the police. It is a policy which is considered by some to be stretching police powers at common law to the hilt if not beyond. In the Dartford Tunnel case the same policy was applied to stop Kent miners some 200 miles away from their destination. An application for an interim injunction, made *ex parte* but on notice to restrain the Chief Constable of Kent from acting unlawfully in obstructing the miners from using the highway and in falsely imprisoning them in the County of Kent was refused (see *The Guardian* 21 March 1984) and the action was not pursued.

It could be argued that if travellers were heading towards private land, such as that in the exclusion order five miles around Stonehenge which some of them were specifically injuncted from entering, then the police could reasonably apprehend a breach of the peace if the owners of

24

that land were prepared to use reasonable force to eject potential trespassers. However, this would only apply to groups of travellers heading towards Stonehenge at the solstice. As set out in the factual summary, many roadblocks were being set up to direct the convoy along a particular route when they were already moving away from Stonehenge. It is difficult to see the justification in law for such roadblocks.

2. Road checks

On several occasions, including 20 June 1985 in the area surrounding Stonehenge and 19 June 1986 surrounding the camp on the 'fish farm' site in Hanging Langford, NCCL observers noted that travellers were being stopped and asked questions in relation to their name, date of birth, place of birth, occupation, colour of eyes, height, address and registration number of car. NCCL observers on the night of 20/21 June in 1985 and 1986 near the Amesbury roundabout were in two successive years asked these questions, the answers to which were entered on a form. It did not appear that the police were using their stop and search powers under the Police and Criminal Evidence Act which are limited to stop searches for stolen goods, aggressive weapons etc. Under section 159 of the Road Traffic Act 1972, a police constable in uniform may stop a motorist or a pedestrian on a road and request drivers to supply their name and address as well as the name and address of the owner, but not require them to change their route. The purpose of these powers is to enable the officer to check the status of the vehicle and if necessary its roadworthiness, and to delay pedestrians for the purpose of traffic control. However, the questions asked, the answers to which were entered on a standard form, appeared to go much further than this power allows, and to be part of a general intelligence gathering exercise. There is no power in law for police officers to stop motor vehicles in order to conduct such an intelligence gathering exercise. The privacy implications of this practice are discussed below.

3. Banning order

A general order was made under S.21 of the Town Police Clauses Act 1847 by the Salisbury District Council in June 1986 banning 'hippies' from the city centre for two specified days to prevent a protest march taking place. The Town Police Clauses Act provisions enable local councils to make orders when the streets are 'thronged or liable to be obstructed' and to direct the police in relation to keeping order and preventing obstruction of the streets in the neighbourhood of theatres and 'other places of public resort'. According to press reports, the concern of the Council was less with any obstruction that might take place than with the declared intention of the marchers to remove their clothes at a specified time. The Town Police Clauses Act was therefore used to limit freedom to demonstrate and protest – a use far from the strict wording of the Act.

4. Road closures

Wiltshire County Council in 1986 refused to join in the injunction proceedings commenced by 25 local landowners (see No Trespassers above). The Council, which had then been of a different political complexion, had been a party to the proceedings in 1985. However, the Chief Constable wrote to the Council requesting that they make an order under S.14 of the Road Traffic Regulation Act 1984. The application was in respect of part of the A34 and various local footpaths. The reasons given by the Chief Constable (see appendix 2) were primarily on the basis that this closure would assist the police, although that is not a ground making an order under S.14 which requires that there be a danger to the public although police suggested there would be danger to the public. The local authority, when making an order as requested, did however state that it was on the basis that there would otherwise be a danger to the public. No danger was specified. In the previous year, the grounds on which English Heritage/National Trust had closed the monument was not that there was any danger to the public, but that there was likely to be damage to the monument. It is difficult to escape the conclusion that the words of the law were being stretched in order to give the police wide discretion to deal with the convoy as they wished. The Act covers dangerous roads and structures on roads rather than 'dangerous' people on the roads.

5. Obstruction

The offence of obstruction of the highway has been one of the main charges in 1986. It is surprising that a relatively minor offence (maximum penalty, a fine of £400) gives rise to wide powers (under certain conditions) for the police to detain and for the courts to impose bail conditions, all of which are very concrete restrictions on the right to freedom of movement. It has often been accompanied by the charge of obstruction of a police officer in the execution of his duty. In law it is an offence for a person without lawful authority or excuse in any way to wilfully obstruct the free passage of the highway.

a. *Obstruction of the Highway*

There is no specific power of arrest, but the general arrest powers in the Police and Criminal Evidence Act 1984 apply. This means that a constable can arrest without warrant where it appears to him/her that service of a summons is impracticable or inappropriate because s/he has 'reasonable grounds for believing that arrest is necessary to prevent the relevant person – causing an unlawful obstruction of the highway' (S. 25 Police and Criminal Evidence Act 1984).

This offence is a serious restriction on any form of public protest. It is one of the most commonly-used charges in public order law and the breadth of the offence is often seen as a *de facto* licensing power over public gatherings.* The police use it to remove sit-down demonstrators,

---

*De Smith *Constitutional & Administrative Law* 3rd Edition page 488

to prevent demonstrators outside South Africa House from straying outside the barrier positions agreed with the police, to keep marchers from leaving the agreed police route, to control pickets and in every conceivable public order context on the highway. There is no requirement of violence or the threat of violence and when cases reach court, prosecutors commonly agree to offer no evidence if the defendant agrees to be bound over – a concession not usually made in more serious cases. In addition the police will sometimes use the charge of obstructing a police officer where a person is obstructing the highway, whether by sitting down, or speaking, or listening, or leafletting, or collecting, and refuses to move on after a police request to do so. The use of the charge in both 1985 and 1986 demonstrates the wide powers it gives to the police to control the movements of unpopular groups despite the fact they are behaving peacefully.

b. *Obstruction of a police officer*

In the aftermath of the police operation on 1 June 1985, approximately 500 people were charged with unlawful assembly, which carries with it a right to trial before a jury. That charge was dropped and almost all defendants were charged with obstruction of the police which is triable before the Magistrates' Court. As the criminal damage was costed at under £400, the individuals concerned were prevented from taking their case before a jury and the cases were triable only in the Magistrates' Court.

A stipendiary magistrate from London, Mr David Miller, spent two weeks in Salisbury Magistrates' Court in October and November 1985, hearing what were generally regarded as test cases on obstruction of the police. The majority of these trials resulted in acquittals on the basis that the prosecution were unable to show any positive act of obstruction by a defendant in the vast majority of cases. The Wiltshire Police successfully appealed to the Divisional Court and, in a judgement given on 16 May 1986, Lord Justice Watkins allowed appeals in three separate sets of cases. The court took the view that a passenger in a vehicle could be held responsible for actions of the driver even where there was no evidence that passengers were encouraging or assisting the driver. There is a line of cases where the courts have taken the view that if anybody is voluntarily with a group where some members commit offences, then the whole group are to be held responsible. This seems to negate the usual burden on the prosecution to prove in each case that an individual has broken the law. It provides encouragement for the police to arrest and charge with obstruction any group of people they want to disperse, regardless of whether they are otherwise committing any offence. Leave to appeal against the decision of the Divisional Court was refused on 26 June 1986. The court took the rather bizarre view that no issue of public importance was involved.

On 20 June 1986 some 230 travellers moving in convoy away from Stonehenge were arrested for obstruction of the highway and obstruction of the police at Hanging Langford. NCCL observers who witnessed some 115 arrests reported that they did not see any obstruction of the highway, prior to the arrests, and that the arrests that they witnessed were peaceful, excessive force was not used by the police, neither did those arrested resist. Although the initial arrests appear to have taken place for obstruction of the highway, charges for obstruction of the police followed. In relation to the alleged obstruction of the highway the travellers were detained for some 18 hours, until they were brought before the courts. Detention for 18 hours seems excessive in relation to an original offence which only carries a fine and does not carry any sentence of imprisonment, and it will be interesting to note when the cases come to court the grounds on which those arrested were detained. It was noted by NCCL observers that convoys had been proceeding along the road for the previous two weeks in a similar manner to that in which they were proceeding on 20 June 1986. However, no arrests took place until the evening of 20 June and the effect of the arrests was to ensure that 230 travellers were off the roads and in custody over the period of the solstice.

6. Bail conditions

Wide ranging bail conditions were imposed by Salisbury magistrates requiring travellers to leave the county of Wiltshire by midnight. Swindon magistrates imposed a similar condition requiring travellers to leave the area as soon as practicable. These conditions caused great difficulty to travellers whose vehicles had been left on the road at Hanging Langford when they were arrested and which were being held in police pound within the county. As the vehicles were being released at a slow rate, many of them were concerned that they would not be able to collect their vehicles and abide by the bail conditions. (*Times* 23 June 1986 and reports of NCCL court observers on 21 June 1986).

Conditions are attached to bail in order to either ensure defendants' presence at court, that he or she does not commit further offences or interfere with witnesses, or obstruct the course of justice, or to ensure that he or she make themselves available for reports.

The magistrates imposed the bail condition because of the likelihood of further offences, yet it was unlikely that there would be further obstruction offences, if only because the relevant vehicles were in police pounds at that time. The practice of imposing wide-ranging bail conditions which amount to a more severe punishment than that which could be imposed if the individual was convicted of the offence with which they had been charged, caused concerned during the miners' dispute. In those cases however, the prosecution stated that such conditions were necessary to avoid further breaches of the peace. In the case of the travellers arrested at Hanging Langford there is no allegation that there was or was likely to be an imminent danger of breach of the peace on the road. The imposition of bail conditions by the magistrates, out of all proportion to the offence of obstruction of the highway, amounts to punishment before trial, still less conviction.

The degree of over-reaction by the police and the courts can perhaps be gauged by the fact that defendants were taken into court, and across a crowded market square on market day, in handcuffs. When challenged by defence solicitors, the police justified the handcuffs on the basis that there was an 'imminent danger of breach of the peace'. After having been addressed by defence lawyers that even those accused of terrorist bombing offences in the Old Bailey the previous week (McGee, O'Dwyer and others) had not been handcuffed in court, the court in Salisbury eventually ordered that handcuffs be removed. This allowed defence solicitors to eventually communicate with their clients.

Public Order Bill

As the above account shows, the police have a wide discretion to use their powers in order to control the activities of the convoy. These powers were introduced by Parliament for a whole variety of different reasons e.g. to ensure the free flow of traffic on the highway, to prevent obstructions around theatres, and to enforce the closure of roads which are a danger to the public. The lack of clear words and a clear codification of public order powers means that laws introduced by Parliament for one purpose, for example, for road traffic control, can be used for another, the dispersal of public assemblies or processions. The Public Order Bill follows this sad tradition by failing to codify the existing law and instead introducing wide powers without safeguards to prevent them being used to discriminate against unpopular minorities such as travellers. Here we give two examples:-
a) The Public Order Bill gives the police new powers to re-route and impose conditions on processions or to decide the duration, location and numbers of public assemblies in the open air on the grounds that they 'seriously disrupt the life of the community'; but which community? If the Bill is passed in its present form next year the police will have powers to limit a moving convoy to two or three vehicles, to break up any groups of 20 or more travellers and to insist that they move from a particular location or leave at a particular time. These powers will apply whether or not the travellers are lawfully on a particular piece of land, and will apply to circumstances where the travellers are behaving perfectly peacefully and there has not been, nor is there any danger of disruption or damage. It assumes that assemblies and travelling groups of people are outside normal community life whereas traditionally the nomadic way of life and the tradition of assembly in the open air has been part of community life.

The power puts the police in the position of deciding between the wishes of different community groups. In 1985 Wiltshire Council, which was Conservative led, took a very proactive approach and joined in injunction proceedings to prevent travellers getting to Stonehenge. The Alliance-controlled Council in 1986 took a lower profile on the issue and did not join in the injunction proceedings, the Salisbury Labour Party called for a properly organised festival as a permanent solution to the police blockade of Stonehenge (*Western Daily Press* 24 June 1986).

However, the travellers are also a 'community' and one that is clearly not represented by the local council who were not elected by people with a nomadic way of life. Should the police then disperse groups of farmers armed with farm implements or shotguns on the grounds that their threatening behaviour disrupts the nomadic way of community life of the travellers? The community living locally in the area of Steeple Langford held a meeting one week after the arrest at Hanging Langford where concern was expressed about the treatment of the travellers – is this *ad hoc* meeting to represent the travellers 'community life'? The church community in the Hampshire and Wiltshire area has played a vocal part in the debates about the convoy. Various churches have also given practical help from welfare assistance to vicars acting as NCCL observers. Are the police to take the comments of people such as Mr Tim Selwood, assistant priest in the Parish of Minstead, near Lindhurst in Hampshire as evidence that the travellers do not 'seriously disrupt community life'?

'It surely is a disgrace that while we have vast tracts of land far from human habitation set aside for the use of the military, and areas like Salisbury Plain happily shared by the military and local people, we are unable as a nation to set aside a few acres as a festival site through which they can pursue their way of life without being a burden on society or traipsing round the country in a huddle of vehicles. Now that the initial over-reaction has passed and those of us living relatively humdrum lives have discovered that we are not threatened by these people at all, surely some government department could make some land available for a few years to see how this phenomenon resolves itself.'

Guardian Letters, 2nd July 1986

Perhaps it is the failure of local and central government to provide sites which is 'seriously disrupting community life'?

Disorderly conduct

The Public Order Bill introduces a new, lower level public order offence. That is, the offence of disorderly conduct which criminalises any threatening, abusive, insulting words or behaviour, or disorderly conduct which causes alarm, harassment or distress. The offence has a two stage power of arrest, similar to the old 'sus' offence. The police first give a warning, and if the behaviour or similar behaviour continues, then the individual can be arrested. The offence has been widely criticised as being open to use in a discriminatory way against unpopular groups, particularly of young people. Loud, boisterous behaviour, unusual banners, badges or posters or displays which could alarm, harass or distress can be penalised by this offence.

The acts complained of do not need to cause injury or damage, or to be likely to cause injury or damage or to be likely to cause a breach of the peace. The offence penalises perfectly peaceful behaviour. Similar offences have been widely used in Commonwealth countries to penalise unpopular views.* For example, a very similarly-worded offence was regularly used against civil rights activists walking down the street with a black person in the 1960s in Mississippi, until the convictions started being overturned by the Supreme Court.

The use of wide and vague powers in a discriminatory way against one group can of itself lead to conflict. The Public Order Bill fails to codify the powers set out above and instead introduces further wide, vague, powers and fails to provide a positive right of assembly.

NCCL believes that the sole criterion for public order control should be a minimum test of actual violence or the immediate threat of violence to persons or property. The threat of violence must be immediate in the sense that it must be proximate in time and place.† Violence must be prevented and the police must have sufficient clear powers in order to do so. However harassment of peaceful travellers should not be allowed either by the new Public Order Bill or the plethora of existing vague powers.

Police confiscation of vehicles

This is an area where the police appear, *prima facie*, to have moved beyond their existing legal powers. Many vehicles have been confiscated by the police and are to be put up for auction if not claimed (*The Guardian*, 25 June 1986). The authority for the confiscation seems to be uncertain. At first the police claimed that they were exercising powers under the Road Traffic Act 1972, although no powers of confiscation (as, for example, in the case of items seized in drugs cases) exists under that Act. The police are entitled to remove a vehicle from the highway if it is an obstruction or if its likely to cause injury, or where the driver has given a positive breath test and there is nobody who can demonstrate the right and the capacity to look after the car. None of these seem to apply to the vehicles taken to the police pound. NCCL of course agrees that untaxed and unroadworthy vehicles should not be allowed on the road. However, we are concerned that in the police operation around Stonehenge on 20/21 June 1985, police seemed to concentrate on stopping young people who looked as though they may be travellers, while vehicles committing road traffic offences passed by unheeded.

In the absence of any clear statement and code of police public order powers and of evidence of an intention in relation to confiscation of vehicles to exceed those powers, it is particularly important that the courts and the Inspector of Constabulary, as well as the police author-ities to whom the police should be accountable, ensure effective supervi-sion and control. As set out above, the courts, by imposing wide ranging

---

*See NCCL briefing *Disorderly Conduct* 1986 Briefing No. 4/2/1986. PO, (£1.50)
†The test is taken from the definition of breach of the peace in the Court of Appeal decision in *Howell* (1982) QB 416 at 427.

bail conditions and failing to enquire into the legality of the police operation in respect of an obstruction of the highway on 20 June 1986, failed to exercise a restraining influence.

The Inspector of Constabulary

In his annual report for 1986 Mr Laurence Byford, HM Inspector of Constabulary describes the police operation on 1 June 1985 as follows:-

> During 1985 the activities of itinerant groups such as the Peace Convoy caused a number of serious public order problems for the police. in particular a violent confrontation took place at Parkhouse in Wiltshire on Saturday 1 June when a convoy of 170 vehicles was being driven toward Stonehenge at the time of the Summer Solstice celebrations, in clear defiance of injunctions which were in force. When the vehicles were stopped by a road-block from proceeding further, they entered nearby fields where a violent confrontation with the police took place and 420 persons were arrested. Such groups as the Peace Convoy, which can be readily distinguished from other 'hippy' type groups who are generally peaceful by nature, now represent a recurring problem for the police and local communities in parts of this country.

It is noteworthy that he fails to mention the considerable criticism of the police operation following televised reports. Further, the Inspector of Constabulary does not comment on the criticism of the police operation by the courts in the case of Reynolds.

As a matter of deliberate policy, very few of the cases arising from the police operation on 1 June 1985 have been heard in the Crown Courts. However, on 6 December 1985, in Salisbury Crown Court, His Honour Starforth Hill heard an appeal in respect of a young woman, Helen Reynolds, who had been convicted in the Magistrates' Court of obstructing a police officer. She had been convicted notwithstanding the fact that photographs were produced at her trial which showed several different police officers smashing the windows of her vehicle (an ambulance) and one police officer attempting to pull her out of her vehicle by her hair through a broken window. Her vehicle had been at the front of the convoy and the police arrested her on the road without her making any attempt to enter the field which the other convoy members entered. In allowing her appeal, the judge specifically stated that he could not see any justification for the way in which the windows of Ms Reynolds' vehicle had been smashed. Approximately 20 cases have been subsequently dropped as a result of the Reynolds' appeal. In spite of the judges comment criminal damage by the police has not been investigated.

Privacy

NCCL observers have been disturbed at the amount of information-gathering taking place in the area of Stonehenge around the solstice. The stopping of people in vehicles in order for officers to complete standard forms seems to be part of such an exercise. It is clear, from an affidavit given in the case brought in the High Court by 25 landowners to obtain an injunction against potential trespassers, that a Stonehenge Intelligence Unit exists. Of course, NCCL accepts that the police need information for the detection of crime and the apprehension of offenders. We are concerned however that information collection and storage is only linked to crimes, also that information on people not suspected of offences should not be stored.

The Data Protection Act 1984 places on the police a duty to keep only information which is accurate, relevant and up to date. We do not know how or for how long information collected by officers at roadchecks is kept. Neither do we know whether information obtained by the Stonehenge Intelligence Unit is relevant and up to date or mere hearsay and gossip. It is to be hoped that the Data Protection Registrar, when scrutinising the application for registration of the Wiltshire Police under the Data Protection Act, ensures that the provisions of the Act are not breached. It is very difficult for a private individual to enforce the Act, as the right of access to computerised information, which will come into force in November 1987, does not include information which is held by police for the prevention or detection of crime or for the apprehension of offenders.

Our concern for the accuracy and relevance of information and that information should not be kept on wholly innocent individuals is based upon practical experience of actual problems experienced by individuals.

Avoiding the Conflict Next Time – the Caravan Sites Act

'A band of medieval brigands who have no respect for law and order and the rights of others.'

Rt. Hon. Douglas Hurd MP, Home Secretary, House of Commons, 3rd June 1986.

There has traditionally been a conflict between travelling people and settled people; between landowners and settled residents on the one hand, and on the other, and gypsies, tinkers, travellers and most recently the 'new age gypsies' such as the convoy. In introducing the Caravan Sites Act in 1968, parliament made it clear that it respected the rights of those with a travelling life-style and made provisions for sites to be provided to avoid the conflict of rights of travellers to roam and of settled people to peaceful enjoyment of their land. This constructive approach is essential if conflict on a yearly basis is to be avoided not least around the solstice period in Hampshire and Wiltshire. Since 1968 the provision of sites has been slow, and despite the events of 1985 (see Factual Summary) local authorities did not provide temporary sites for the convoy nor did the Secretary of State for the Environment use his powers to do so. Instead, both central and local government sat back and waited for the police to use their public order powers to deal with the inevitable conflict.

All people of nomadic habit of life leaving aside specific exemptions in the Act should be recognised as deserving of sites within the terms of the Act. The lack of provision of adequate sites for travellers to stay on has been at the heart of the peace convoy's problems. It is clear that there has been a failure to provide adequate sites for travellers in general. The Department of the Environment itself has estimated that sites are only provided for some 40% of travellers. The solution lies in the Caravan Sites Act 1968. The Act provides that it is the duty of every local authority county or borough to provide sites with adequate accommodation for gypsies defined in the Caravan Sites Act as 'persons of nomadic habit of life', whatever their race or origin. This would appear to include the members of the peace convoy. The only exception specified in the Caravan Sites Act is members of an organised group of travelling showmen or persons engaged in travelling circuses. But many local authorities, usually in response to local resentment, have failed to provide sites, even emergency sites, and have passed the problem back to the police. If local authorities do avoid their responsibilities, the Caravan Sites Act provides a procedure to force them by way of *mandamus* in the High Court to comply, and also gives the Secretary of State for the Environment the power to direct that sites are provided. In no case has the Secretary of State issued any such direction (Hansard, 18 June 1986, Written Answer No. 86).

'Real gypsies'

It is ironic for the Home Secretary to idealise 'real gypsies' when they are the focus of as much prejudice and harassment as the 'new age' gypsies of the convoy. 'Egyptians', as Henry VIII's legislation against aliens defined them in the 1540s, were subject then to the death penalty. Not only did that Act stay on the statute book until well into the 19th century, but many gypsies were persecuted under it, including a large number who were hanged in York in 1677. Even in this century Romany families complained of constant police harassment under the successive Highways Acts from 1835 to 1980, which made it an offence for a person 'being a gypsy' to encamp on the highway, and that usually includes the verge. Romany families will still tell of needing shutters on their caravans to protect themselves from stoning by locals in a new area to which they had moved. The Commission for Racial Equality accepts gypsies as a 'racial group' for the purposes of civil law following the leading case *Mandla v Singh*. Moreover, they are pressing the government to include gypsies as a racial group for the purposes of incitement to racial hatred under the Public Order Act 1986. The reason for the amendment put forward by the Commission for Racial Equality is the large amount of abusive threatening and racist material they receive in relation to gypsies.

As at January 1986 a total of 10,592 gypsy caravans were recorded (Hansard, 18 June 1986, Written Answer No. 82-85). There were only approximately 4,000 places for those caravans. Thus only about 40 per cent of gypsy families have a legal pitch to stop on. Hampshire in particular is still very short of site provision for traveller families. All local authorities and police in Dorset and most of Wiltshire can prosecute and evict *any* gypsy family which stops on highways, vacant land or occupied land without the occupier's consent – under what are called designation orders granted under the Caravan Sites Act 1968. (See below).

What is a gypsy?

Are any or all of the convoy members 'gypsies' under the Caravan Sites Act 1968? This is an important question, and one which shows confusion amongst many people who debate it. 'Persons of nomadic habit of life, whatever their race or origin, other than a group of travelling showmen, travelling together as such' is the exact definition in S. 16 of the Act. It is vital to note that this is a definition by lifestyle: racial or other origin is specifically excluded from the calculation. Clearly rights and responsibilities for providing facilities for accommodating travellers do not and should not depend on racial origin.

★ ★ ★

Caravan Sites Act 1968

The Caravan Sites Act 1968 as amended puts a legal duty on:-
–each shire county to provide 'adequate accommodation' for gypsies 'residing or resorting to their area'
–each London Borough and each District council in the six former metropolitan counties to provide sites for '15 caravans at a time'.

Designation

The reward for 'adequate accommodation' is in the power of the Secretary of State for the Environment. It is called 'designation' and it enables the local authorities and police in a 'designated area' to prosecute gypsies who are not stopping on legal sites. So if Travellers are on highway verges, 'unoccupied land' or 'occupied land' without the consent of the occupier, they can be prosecuted quickly in the Magistrates' Court, and the local authority can then get an order to evict all the caravans.

Carrot and Stick

The philosophy behind the Caravan Sites Act has been called the 'carrot and stick'. The assumption was that local authorities would not wish to provide sites for gypsies, so the carrot of 'designation' (see above) would be dangled in front of them as a reward. Originally 'designation' could only be granted to whole counties, but since 1980, individual districts can get it, if the county and the district apply jointly.

The 'stick' was the Environment Minister's power to instruct an authority to provide a site if they dragged their feet. Although these powers were retained by amending legislation in 1980, the Environment Secretary in England is lagging behind his Welsh counterpart. West Glamorgan was instructed to provide sites, including the notoriously anti-gypsy area of Swansea, in April 1986.

In spite of appalling site shortages in such counties as Avon, Hereford and Worcester, the English minister has yet to issue *any* direction under the Act.

The carrot and stick mentality is arguably racist, and exists for no other minority needing accommodation. 'Designation' is becoming a live issue with those who work with Travellers as much as with Travellers themselves. Shouldn't it be swept away?

According to Mr Richard Tracey, Minster of State at the Department of the Environment (Hansard, 18 June 1986, Written Answer No. 172), groups such as the peace convoy are not normally included in the Department's estimate of caravans belonging to individuals whom the authorities accept as of the nomadic habit of life referred to in the Caravan Sites Act 1968. However, many members of the convoy are, according to their own detailed accounts given to NCCL observers, of a nomadic habit of life. Depending upon their individual circumstances they have a strong claim to site provision under the Caravan Sites Act. If that claim is accepted or legally upheld, convoy members would, however, also face the sanctions of prosecution and eviction for illegal parking in areas covered by designation orders under the 1968 Act. (See above)

Although most of the comment received by NCCL in relation to the convoy was (as one might expect from people telephoning an organisation such as NCCL) in favour of the travellers' right to lead a nomadic life style, a few members of the public took the view that nothing positive should be done for those who live a different life style, not paying rent or rates. Such an attitude relates to publicity which has surrounded the convoy and may explain the antipathetic approach of some local MPs. However, in passing the 1968 Act, Parliament was confirming that a nomadic lifestyle is legitimate and that, if a conflict of interest between nomads and the house dwellers is to be avoided, sites need to be provided.

If the convoy and similar groups are to obtain legal accommodation under the Caravan Sites Act, for wintering facilities for their living vehicles, then the whole machinery of the 1968 Act must be brought into play for the whole travelling population of which the convoy is a part. The Select Committee on the Environment, in its July 1985 report, expressed great concern over the 'slow rate of provision of gypsy caravan sites' and asked for a policy review by the government department responsible. That 'modest review' accepted some 70 submissions by 31 March 1986 and the resulting report is eagerly awaited. Bearing in mind the flurry of publicity over the convoy and the outstanding and urgent needs of more traditional travellers, the Department of the Environment must carry out its duty.

A solution to the recurring problem of travellers converging on Stonehenge area at the solstice should not be separated from the pressing need to reassess the lack of effectiveness of the Caravan Sites Act. The mechanism of designation should not prevent local authorities from providing specific sites on a temporary basis when there is a sudden influx, or permanent sites when the number of travellers in their area increases. Designation is a recognition of provision at a specific point of time. The Act does not state that a designated level is a permanent level and indeed in May 1986, for example, Kent County Council was in the process of providing more sites than the 30 designated in Tonbridge and Medway because there had been an increase in population in that area. An increase in population which is predictable on an annual basis should lead to a provision of appropriate site – failure to do so will make conflict inevitable.

Conclusion

1. Prior to the summer solstice of 1985 and 1986 Britain was in the grip of a moral panic. Travellers to Stonehenge were folk devils, and stories about the threatening life style of the 'hippies' abounded in the press and in Parliament. In this report we have questioned the allegations that the convoy was disease ridden, dangerous, and lawless; and have not found the allegations to be backed by evidence. The treatment of these travellers by the media, politicians and police show how easily the civil liberties of an unpopular minority can be swept aside.

There has traditionally been a conflict between travelling people and settled people. In the Caravan Sites Act 1968, parliament recognised the legitimacy of a nomadic way of life but decided that, in order to avoid conflict between travelling people and settled people, Local Authorities were to be given a duty to provide sites for people of a nomadic way of life. This should include the convoy. However less than half of gypsy families recorded by local councils have been provided with official sites. Counties such as Hampshire have failed in their duty under the Act. Central government in the person of the Secretary of State for the

Environment has the power to direct them to fulfil their legal obligations but has not done so. NCCL recommends that adequate provision of sites with proper facilities is made for all travellers. It has been noticeable that the media and parliament have chosen to level their criticism at the convoy rather than Local Authorities or the Department of the Environment for their failure to deal with the problem.

2. There have also been negotiations about providing a temporary site for a festival at Stonehenge over the solstice. While we would not suggest that temporary sites should always be found for any number of people who wish to hold a festival, we recommend that a site is found near Stonehenge in June 1987 for the following reasons: First, the freedom to assemble is a hollow freedom if there is no open space on which to exercise it. With the shrinking of common land the provision of temporary sites for public assemblies such as festivals run noncommercially must fall on public authorities. Second, the provision of a temporary site will lessen any danger of a breach of the peace, mass trespass and conflicts such as those described in this booklet.

3. The failure of central and local government has meant that the police were left with the job of dealing with large groups of people going towards Stonehenge. Because there are insufficient legal sites for the convoy to go to, the police had the role of evicting the convoy from non-legal sites and then dispersing them, using methods some of which exceeded their legal powers. The police used their common law powers to prevent a breach of the peace, and a wide range of powers introduced by Parliament for a variety of reasons from controlling road traffic (obstruction of the highway) to disrupting throngs outside theatres (Town Police Clauses Act). These vague powers are interpreted widely by the courts, for example convictions for obstruction of the highway are regularly upheld when used to disperse demonstrations and even passive passengers in vehicles have been convicted of the offence of obstruction of a police officer. The need for a clear code of public order powers, so that both the individual citizen and the police officer are aware of their rights and duties is demonstrated by the confusion of the travellers, and the sometimes contradictory explanations by the police of their use of road blocks, road checks and traffic offences. In this confusion, the rights of an unpopular minority can easily be swept aside.

4. The Public Order Bill presently before parliament fails to codify public order law, but instead introduces new powers for the police to impose conditions on processions and assemblies in the open air. For example the police will be able to move on a group of say 20 travellers from common land, where they have a right to be at present, on the grounds that they 'seriously disrupt the life of the community'. But who is the community? In this report we have shown that in the local area there was a whole range of attitudes toward the convoy, which differed from political party to political party, between clergy and local farmers, and from landowner to landowner. The convoy itself is also a travelling community, and their community life was seriously disrupted by the action of landowners and police.

5. The consequence of treating assemblies as outside community life, instead of part of our democratic tradition, is to make the police arbiters of what is normal and what is disruptive, without their being accountable to any democratically-elected body for this operational decision. The police exercised wide discretion in their control of the convoy and are not accountable to the courts for their operational decisions, unless someone charged with a criminal offence puts forward the claim that the police exceeded their powers. Neither do the police authorities have any control over police operations. It is notable that the police authorities in Wiltshire and Hampshire have been largely silent about the police operation.

6. The Public Order Bill does not include safeguards to prevent the new powers being used in a discriminatory manner against unpopular minorities. In this report, we have found several instances of the police concentrating for example on stopping young 'convoy type' people near Stonehenge and ignoring other vehicles committing Road Traffic offences, of charging travellers with obstruction offences but failing to enforce the law against farmers who blocked off roads. The introduction of new, lower-level public order powers such as disorderly conduct, i.e. a new criminal offence of using threatening, abusive, insulting or disorderly words or behaviour likely to cause alarm, harassment or distress, will open the way to harassment of unpopular minorities, just as the 'Sus' law was used against young black people.

7. We have considered whether there is a need for a new criminal trespass law. Farmer Attwell for example faced real difficulties in removing travellers from his land, whom he said damaged his land and therefore his livelihood. However his problem stemmed from lack of funds and procedural difficulties, which slowed down what should be a fast and effective civil remedy. The solution may lie in making the law more accessible, by changing the eligibility limits for legal aid to persons in Mr Attwell's position. The current wording of the proposed new offence of criminal trespass, (to be inserted into the Public Order Bill), is so worded that it would penalise not only travellers but ramblers and birdwatchers and bring neighbour disputes into the criminal courts. It is notable that the police failed to use their existing criminal powers to assist farmer Attwell before the order was granted by the civil court.

8. The Public Order Bill is part of a trend by government to treat deep-seated conflicts between different groups in society, whether they be workers and employers or travellers and settled people, as primarily public order problems. Thus government avoids fulfilling its responsibilities to mediate between the parties and avoid conflict, in this case by providing a site for travellers and at Stonehenge. The police are again put in the front line and are stretching, at times over-reaching their legal powers to deal with the conflict which inevitably ensues. In this way, our civil liberties, our freedom of assembly and freedom of movement are disappearing. First by attempts to 'neutralise' an unpopular minority of travellers and then, through the Public Order Bill, to limit all peaceful demonstrations. The use of such powers will not prevent travellers

attempting to reach Stonehenge in June 1987, but will ensure harassment, alarm and distress not only for the convoy but also for the settled residents of the area.

The solution is for government to take up its responsibility to resolve this clash of interests through peaceful means, rather than characterising it as a law and order issue.

NCCL recommends that:

1. The government should reaffirm its recognition of the legitimacy of people having a nomadic lifestyle.
2. The government should remind Local Authorities of their duty to provide adequate sites under the 1968 Caravan Sites Act.
3. Where a Local Authority fails to carry out its duty the Secretary of State for the Environment should use his powers to ensure that the Local Authority makes sites available.
4. A special provision should be made near Stonehenge for a festival site at the solstice in order to allow freedom of assembly and to prevent the conflicts in 1985 and 1986 reoccuring.
5. The government should make considerations on how the procedures in relation to trespass as a civil offence can be made easier – in the light of farmer Attwell's experience.
6. Trespass should not be made a criminal offence.
7. Public order law should be codified and redrafted to include a statutory right to freedom of speech and assembly.
8. The police should be made fully accountable to elected representatives for their policing, priorities, policies and methods.

APPENDIX 1

Parliamentary Question

HOUSE OF COMMONS

Mr Clive Soley (Lab – Hammersmith): To ask the Secretary of State for the Environment, which local authorities are designated under the Caravan Sites Act 1968.

Richard Tracey

The following local authority areas have been designated:-

London Boroughs
Barking, Bexley, Camden, Croydon, Enfield, Greenwich, Hammersmith & Fulham, Havering, Hillingdon, Islington, Kensington & Chelsea, Kingston-upon-Thames, Lambeth, Lewisham, Merton, Newham, Redbridge, Richmond-upon-Thames, Sutton, Waltham Forest, Wandsworth, Westminster.

Metropolitan Districts
Oldham, Trafford, Rochdale.

Areas of former County Boroughs
Bolton, Bury, Leeds, Lincoln, Manchester, Oxford, Plymouth, St Helens, Stoke-on-Trent, Wolverhampton.

Counties and Districts
Bedfordshire:- Luton, South Bedfordshire.
Berkshire:- Windsor & Maidenhead.
Buckinghamshire:- Aylesbury Vale, Chiltern, Milton Keynes, South Bucks.
Cambridgeshire:- Huntingdonshire, Peterborough.
Cheshire:- Chester.
Cleveland:- Hartlepool, Middlesborough, Stockton-on-Tees,
Derbyshire:- Bolsover, Chesterfield, High Peak, North East Derbyshire, South Derbyshire.
Dorest – whole county.
East Sussex:- Eastbourne, Hastings, Rother, Wealden.
Hertfordshire:- Broxbourne.
Kent:- Ashford, Dartford, Gravesham, Tonbridge & Malling.
Lancashire:- Hyndburn.
Lincolnshire:- Boston, West Lindsey.
Northamptonshire:- Northampton, South Northamptonshire, Wellingborough.
North Yorkshire:- Selby.
Shropshire:- Oswestry.
Suffolk:- Babergh, Ipswich, Mid-Suffolk, Suffolk Coastal.
Surrey:- Epsom & Ewell.
Warwickshire:- Nuneaton & Bedworth.
West Sussex – whole county.
Wiltshire – whole county.

Wednesday 18 June 1986 for
Friday 13 June 1986 (No 83)
Department of the Environment   3185/85/86
                                                      (28)

APPENDIX 2

WILTSHIRE CONSTABULARY

POLICE HEADQUARTERS,
DEVIZES,
SN10 2DN.
Telephone: 0380 2241
Telex: 44206

All Communications should be addressed to the Chief Constable.

Your Reference

Our Reference RCD/SKL/SS

Date 19th June, 1986

SUMMER SOLSTICE CEREMONY - STONEHENGE

I well understand the desire of certain groups of persons wishing to conduct a ceremony in the vicinity of Stonehenge at sunrise on the 21st June. My first duty must be to ensure that the peace is preserved and provided I can be satisfied that there will be no Breach of the Peace, I am prepared to allow a limited ceremony to take place. This will be subject to the following conditions:-

1. That the persons as a group now camped at Steeple Langford are not permitted to attend.

2. That a maximum of 300 persons will be permitted.

3. That these 300 persons be properly organised, orderly, and controlled and that once the ceremony has taken place, the group will disperse and leave the area. It is further understood that the ceremony will commence at dawn and conclude no later than 0700 hours, 21st June, 1986. Each individual ceremony must not take longer than 45 minutes.

4. That the 300 persons travel to the area in privately contracted coaches, the firm or firms used to be previously identified to the Police and that they travel to a location previously identified by the Police.

5. Having reached the previously identified location, groups of 100 will be permitted to travel to the junction of the A303 and A344 where all persons

/Cont'd....

- 2 -

will dismount, hold their ceremony and return to the coaches and travel back to the assembly point. This procedure to be repeated on 3 occasions to allow all 300 to have their ceremony.

6. That at any time in the process, the agreement may be suspended or cancelled if the senior police officer present fears that a Breach of the Peace has or is about to develop by reason of either those 300 attending or others who may be approaching the area. Should a Breach of the Peace occur, the Police will expect all in the vicinity to assist in quelling the disturbance.

Chief Constable,
(D. SMITH)

To:

Mr. B. OUBRIDGE
Mr. D. AITKEN and others

APPENDIX 3

the other criteria for assistance under that Act before such a
duty could arise in relation to them. All these matters are for
the appropriate local authorities to decide in the light of the
facts of each case.

Yours sincerely

Paul Heron

PAUL HERON
Private Secretary

2F

PJ

DEPARTMENT OF THE ENVIRONMENT
2 MARSHAM STREET LONDON SW1P 3EB
01-212 3434

My ref: R/PSO/15321/86
Your ref:

27th June 1986

Ms Sarah Spencer
General Secretary
National Council for Civil Liberties
21 Tabard Street
London
SE1 4LA

Dear Ms Spencer

I am replying, on behalf of Mr Tracey, to your letter to the
Prime Minister of 3 June on the subject of the Peace Convoy.
Since you wrote there has been much public airing of the complex
issues involved. On 3 June the Home Secretary replied to
Parliamentary questions concerning the Convoy.

In your letter you raise the question of the provision of
suitable sites for the Peace Convoy under the Caravan Sites
Act 1968. That legislation was designed to deal with the
provision by local authorities, so far as may be necessary, of
adequate accommodation for gipsies residing or resorting to
their areas. I should emphasise that the Act is concerned
with the provision of caravan sites not tenting and camping
sites. To the extent that individuals in the Peace Convoy were
to seek accommodation under the Act, it would be for the
appropriate local authority to consider the facts of the
particular case and to determine whether they qualified for
assistance. In the case of those with caravans, who were
accepted by the authority concerned as being of 'nomadic habit
of life', it would be for that authority to consider whether
the individuals concerned 'resided in or resorted to' the
authority's area, within the meaning of the Act. That judgement
would involve the consideration of the pattern of residence
in, or resorting to, that authority's area. A sudden and
unexpected influx of gipsies into an authority's area would not,
in the Department's view, be sufficient to impose a statutory
duty on that authority under the Act.

I have set out the position in some detail in order to illustrate
the main point, that it is not considered that there is any
duty under the 1968 Act for local authorities to provide a site
or sites specifically for the Peace Convoy as a group.
Individuals in the Convoy would need to establish that they
were gipsies (within the meaning of that Act) and satisfy

1

This is 100% recycled paper